Floating and Sinking

Karen Bryant-Mole

First published in Great Britain by Heinemann Library, Halley Court, Jordan Hill, Oxford OX2 8EJ
a division of Reed Educational & Professional Publishing Ltd.

OXFORD FLORENCE PRAGUE MADRID ATHENS MELBOURNE AUCKLAND KUALA LUMPUR
SINGAPORE TOKYO IBADAN NAIROBI KAMPALA JOHANNESBURG GABORONE PORTSMOUTH
NH (USA) CHICAGO MEXICO CITY SAO PAULO

Designed by Jean Wheeler
Commissioned photography by Zul Mukhida
Consultant – Hazel Grice
Printed in Hong Kong / China

02 01 00 99 98
10 9 8 7 6 5 4 3 2 1

ISBN 0 431 07831 9

British Library Cataloguing in Publication Data

Bryant-Mole, Karen
   Floating and sinking. - (Science all around me)
   1. Hydrostatics - Juvenile literature
   I. Title
   532.2'5

A number of questions are posed in this book. They are designed
to consolidate children's understanding by encouraging further
exploration of the science in their everyday lives.

**Words that appear in the text in bold can
be found in the glossary.**

Acknowledgements
The Publishers would like to thank the following for permission to reproduce photographs: Eye Ubiquitous 4, (S. Greenland),
16 (A. Cudbertson); Positive Images 6, 8, 10, 18, 20; Tony Stone Images 14 (David Schultz); Zefa 22.

Every effort had been made to contact copyright holders of any material reproduced in this book. Any omissions will be
rectified in subsequent printings if notice is given to the Publisher.

Contents

Floating

The boy in this boat is moving through water without getting wet. This is because his boat floats.

Anything that stays at the top of water is said to float.

ⓘ *Small sailing boats are called dinghies.*

See for yourself ...

Emerich wanted to find some things that could float.

He tested lots of different things by placing them in a bowl of water.

He found five things that could float.

Sinking

When something that cannot float is put into water, it sinks.

This **anchor** can't float. It has sunk to the bottom of the water.

? *What do you think might be on the other end of the chain?*

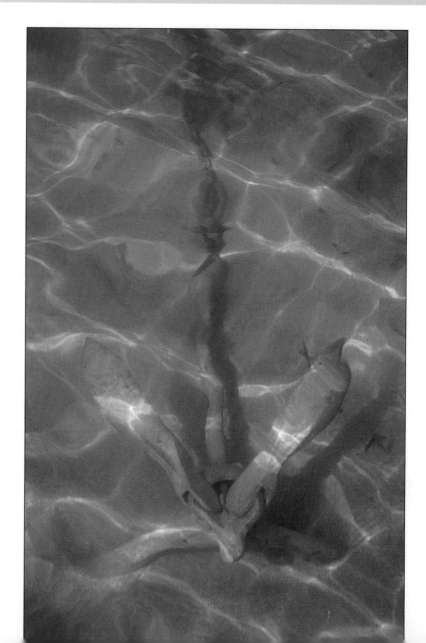

See for yourself ...

Melissa is testing some things to see which float and which sink.

She has put them into two groups. Can you guess which group floats and which group sinks?

Emerich's test will give you a clue!

Size

What makes some things float and some things sink? Size could be important. But look, this large boat and this small boat both float.

(i) *A large stone and a small stone would both sink.*

See for yourself ...

Jessica has done a test with objects that are about the same size and shape.

She has discovered that some float and some sink.

Size might be important but it can't be the only thing that matters.

Heaviness

Whether or not something can float could be to do with how much it **weighs**.

Heavy things might sink and light things might float.

But look, both this log and these leaves float.

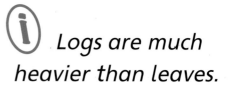 *Logs are much heavier than leaves.*

See for yourself ...

Adam is testing some objects that all weigh about the same.

He thought they would all float or all sink. But some float and some sink.

Weight might be important but it can't be the only thing that matters.

Pushing water

To understand why things float, we need to know what happens when something is put into water.

When the plates were put into this washing-up bowl, they pushed the water out of the way to make space for themselves.

This is called displacement.

? *Where do you think the displaced water has gone?*

See for yourself ...

Alex carefully filled two jugs with water.

She put a large stone into one jug. Water was displaced into a beaker in front of the jug.

When she tried this with a smaller stone, less water was displaced.

Water pushes back

As these tree trunks roll into the water, they push the water out of the way to make room for themselves.

The water pushes back, trying to get back into the space it was in.

(i) *If the water pushes back strongly enough, an object will float.*

See for yourself ...

Jonathan put a table tennis ball into a glass of water.

He is trying to push it down under the water.

He can feel the water that is being pushed out of the way, pushing back.

Under the water

This boat has been taken out of the water.

You can see that much of the boat is usually under the water. The boat is a big shape for the water to push against.

(i) *The more of something there is for water to push against, the more likely it is to float.*

Emerich found two pieces of Plasticine that were both the same weight.

He rolled one into a ball. He made the other into a boat shape.

The ball-shaped piece sinks. The boat-shaped piece floats because the plasticine is spread out into a big shape. There is more Plasticine for the water to push against.

17

Materials

Whether something floats or sinks depends on both its weight and its size.

This windsurf board is big but it is very light and so it floats.

(i) *Something that is light for its size is more likely to float than something that is heavy for its size.*

See for yourself ...

Holly found that the material that things are made of is important.

Things made of solid wood or polystyrene seem to float more easily than things made of solid metal or stone.

Air

This huge ship is made of metal.

If it was made of solid metal it would sink. But most of the space inside the ship is full of air.

(i) *Air makes things light for their size and helps them to float.*

See for yourself ...

Edward is testing some bath toys.

He has found that many of them are hollow.

Hollow things aren't empty. They are full of air.

Waterproof

Some **materials** **soak up** water.

If something soaks up a lot of water, it may sink.

This boat has special paint on it. It stops the water soaking into the wood underneath.

(i) *Materials that do not soak up water are 'waterproof'.*

See for yourself ...

Alex floated pieces of cardboard, **fabric**, plastic and foil on water.

She wanted to find out which materials were waterproof.

A few hours later, both the cardboard and the fabric had soaked up water and sunk.

Glossary

anchor a heavy metal object, used to keep boats in place

fabric cloth

material what things are made from

soak up suck up

solid the same all the way through, not hollow

weighs how heavy something is

Index